YOUNG'S SEAFOOD
COOKBOOK

Colour Library Books

INTRODUCTION

Seafood is one of the most versatile and exciting foods which can be eaten in a wide range of starter or main course meals. In line with today's guidelines on healthy eating, seafood is high in protein, yet low in fat and comes in a variety of tastes and textures.

An increase in foreign travel in recent years has led to tastes for seafood becoming more adventurous, and advanced fishing methods have meant that a much wider selection of fish and shell-fish is now available to cater for that demand. Seafood lovers are now able to explore new tastes and recipes as well as still enjoying the best of the traditional seafood favourites.

In addition, modern freezing methods now allow fish that has been caught in its seasonal prime to be on sale all year round.

Young's offer a wide range of seafood that is selected only from the very best catches and in the following pages they have created a number of recipes for every eating occasion. Where possible they have included tips and easy preparation methods to show how easy it is to enjoy seafood.

Young's have over 150 years of experience in bringing the best seafood to your homes. So whether you're choosing prawns for cocktails or lobster for dressing, you can rely on Young's for top quality frozen speciality seafood all year round.

CLB 2687
© 1991 Colour Library Books Ltd., Godalming, Surrey.
Printed in Singapore.
All rights reserved.
ISBN 0 86283 869 X

The Young's Seafood logo is the registered
trademark of UB (Ross-Young) Ltd.

SMOKED SALMON AND EGG FLAN

SERVES 4-6

This sophisticated flan is versatile enough for any occasion.

Short Crust Pastry
300g/10oz plain flour
Pinch salt
150g/5oz butter
Water to mix

85g/3oz Young's Scottish Smoked Salmon Slices, defrosted
3 tomatoes, peeled and chopped
4 eggs
124ml/¼ pint single cream
Salt and pepper
2 tsps chopped parsley or chives
Tomato and chives for garnish

1. Mix together the flour and salt and rub in butter in a large mixing bowl, until the mixture resembles fine breadcrumbs.

2. Make a well in the centre of mixture and add enough water to make a firm dough. Chill the dough for at least 30 minutes.

STEP 2

3. Roll out pastry and use to line an 20cm (8-inch) flan dish.

4. Chop the salmon into small pieces and place in the pastry case with the chopped tomatoes. Beat together the eggs and cream.

STEP 4

5. Add salt and pepper and stir in chives or parsley. Pour this into the flan.

6. Place dish on a baking tray and bake in preheated oven at 200°C/400°F/Gas Mark 6 for 35-40 minutes until filling is set. Garnish with tomato and chives before serving.

STEP 5

Cook's Notes

TIME: Preparation takes about 15 minutes and cooking about 35-40 minutes.

SERVING IDEA: Ideal for a starter or main meal. Serve warm or cold.

LEMON MARINADED SARDINES

SERVES 4

This delicate blend of ingredients will prompt numerous compliments.

90ml/6 tbsps lemon juice
2.5g/½ tsp paprika
30ml/2 tbsps olive oil
2 bay leaves
2.5g/½ tsp salt
Black pepper
1 onion
1 clove garlic
454g/1lb Young's Sardines
1 lemon to garnish

1. Mix together the lemon juice, paprika, olive oil, bay leaves and salt and pepper.

2. Chop the onion very finely. Crush the garlic.

3. Add onion and garlic to the lemon mixture.

4. Arrange the sardines in a dish, pour the marinade over and cover with clingfilm.

STEP 4

5. Refrigerate for 2-4 hours, turning occasionally.

6. Remove the sardines from the marinade and barbecue or grill under medium heat until the skin just begins to brown.

STEP 3

STEP 6

Cook's Notes

TIME: Preparation takes about 15 minutes plus 2-4 hours for marinating. Cooking takes 10-15 minutes.

VARIATION: The sardines can also be cooked under a medium grill or fried gently, with a little oil.

SERVING IDEA: Garnish with lemon wedges, lemon zest strips and parsley sprigs.

GOLDEN PRAWNS WITH STIR-FRY VEGETABLES

SERVES 4

This imaginative combination of ingredients results in the perfect lunch or supper dish.

100g/4oz small carrots
150g/6oz courgettes
100g/4oz mange tout
150g/6oz baby sweetcorn
400g/14oz Young's Golden King Prawns
30ml/2 tbsps oil
1 garlic clove, crushed (optional)
2.5g/½ tsp finely chopped fresh ginger
Fresh coriander to garnish

1. Wash and drain the vegetables. Using a potato peeler or mandolin, cut the carrots and courgettes into wafer thin wide strips. Top and tail the mange tout. Split the sweetcorn in two down the centre.

STEP 1

2. Cook the prawns according to the pack instructions.

STEP 2

3. Meanwhile, heat the oil in a wok or large frying pan. Add the garlic and ginger if used.

4. Quickly stir-fry the vegetables in the oil until hot, but still crunchy.

STEP 4

5. Pile vegetables into a serving dish. Pile the hot prawns on top and serve at once, garnished with sprigs of fresh coriander.

Cook's Notes

TIME: Preparing the vegetables takes about 10 minutes, cooking takes about 15 minutes.

LOBSTER NEWBURG
SERVES 2

Lobster is perfectly complemented by pepper and cream in this tasty dish.

1 Young's Lobster, defrosted
25g/1oz butter
30ml/2 tbsps sherry or Madeira
2 egg yolks, beaten
Pinch white pepper
Pinch cayenne pepper
2.5ml/½ tsp paprika
75ml/5 tbsps single cream

STEP 2

1. Cut the lobster in half lengthwise. Carefully detach the tail meat and slice it thinly. Crack the claws and remove the meat.

3. Pour the sherry or Madeira over and cool quickly to reduce the liquor by half.

4. Beat egg yolks, seasoning and cream together.

5. Add to the pan and stir, off the heat. Reheat very gently until the cream mixture reaches a sauce consistency. Do not overheat.

STEP 1

2. Melt the butter in a frying pan. Add the lobster, cook for 1-2 minutes.

STEP 5

Cook's Notes

⏲ TIME: Preparation takes about 10 minutes, plus another 10 minutes for cooking.

◯ SERVING IDEA: Serve on a bed of rice, or with large heart shaped croutes.

SUMMER PRAWN CHOWDER

SERVES 4

A creamy, delicate soup, perfect for dinner parties.

12g/½oz fresh root ginger
1 clove garlic
1½ pints double cream
1 large webb, cos or iceberg lettuce
25g/1oz butter or polyunsaturated margarine
600ml/1 pint fish or vegetable stock
340g/12oz Young's Cooking Prawns, defrosted

2. Shred the lettuce. Melt the butter in a large, heavy-based pan.

STEP 2

1. Peel the ginger and chop very finely. Peel and crush the garlic. Infuse these in the cream for one hour.

STEP 1

3. Add lettuce and stir-fry for 1 minute only. Add cream mixture, fish or vegetable stock and the prawns. Cook for 2-3 minutes only.

STEP 3

Cook's Notes

⏱ TIME: Preparation takes about 10 minutes, plus one hour for garlic and ginger to infuse in cream. Cooking takes approximately 5 minutes.

◯ SERVING IDEA: Pour into soup bowls and serve at once with lots of crusty bread.

TROUT TERYAKI

SERVES 2

A delightfully different recipe which is sure to become a favourite.

2 Young's Rainbow Trout, defrosted
4 spring onions, cut in half and sliced lengthways
Zest of half an orange, cut off in strips and thinly sliced
2.5cm/1-inch slice fresh root ginger, cut into slivers
1 small carrot, sliced lengthways and cut into thin strips
150ml/¼ pint soy sauce
Freshly ground black pepper
150ml/¼ pint dry white wine

1. Place trout in a large frying pan and add all remaining ingredients. Cover with a lid and bring mixture to the boil.

STEP 1

2. Reduce heat and simmer for 10-15 minutes until cooked through. Transfer the trout to a serving plate. Spoon the julienne vegetables and the cooking liquor over the top.

Slicing vegetables

STEP 2

Cook's Notes

⏱ TIME: Preparation takes about 10 minutes, plus cooking time of 15-20 minutes.

◯ SERVING IDEA: Serve with new potatoes.

TROUT WITH FENNEL

SERVES 6

Impress your guests with this simple, yet delicious dish.

6 Young's Rainbow Trout, defrosted
50ml/4 tbsps sunflower oil
1 small fennel bulb, sliced
Salt and freshly ground pepper
Sprigs of fresh fennel to garnish
6 slices of lemon
6 sprigs fresh fennel

STEP 2

1. Snip off the fins from the trout and make two or three slashes on both sides of each trout. Lay them in a shallow dish.

3. When ready to cook, lift the trout out of the marinade and place a sprig of fennel and a slice of lemon inside each one.

STEP 1

STEP 3

2. Mix together the oil, sliced fennel and seasoning and pour over the trout. Cover and chill for 2 hours, turning once.

4. Cook on a moderately hot barbecue for about 10 minutes, turning the trout over halfway through cooking and basting occasionally with the marinade. Garnish with fresh fennel and serve hot.

Cook's Notes

⏰ TIME: 10 minutes for preparation, plus 2 hours for marinating and 10 minutes for cooking.

❓ VARIATION: Can be grilled for about 10 minutes instead of barbecued.

🔲 SERVING IDEA: Serve warm with salad.

CHARCOAL GRILLED SARDINES WITH HOT TOMATO SAUCE

SERVES 6

These appetising little fish are perfect for summer barbecues.

425g/15oz can chopped tomatoes
30ml/2 tbsps tomato purée
1 garlic clove, crushed
2.5ml/½ tsp chilli sauce
1 spring onion, finely sliced
1 tbsp chopped fresh parsley
60ml/4 tbsps olive oil
Salt and freshly ground pepper
3 × 454g Young's Sardines, defrosted
Slices of lemon and sprigs of dill to garnish

STEP 1

1. Mix the tomatoes, tomato purée, garlic and chilli sauce in a food processor or blender and process until almost smooth. Stir in spring onions, parsley and seasoning.

2. Brush the sardines with oil and cook on a moderately hot barbecue for about 8 minutes until the skin chars slightly, turning over halfway through cooking and basting occasionally with the tomato sauce.

3. Serve the sardines at once, garnished with lemon and dill, and the rest of the tomato sauce.

STEP 1

STEP 3

Cook's Notes

⏱ TIME: Preparation takes about 5 minutes, plus 8-10 minutes for barbecuing.

❓ VARIATION: Can also be cooked under a medium grill for 8 minutes.

SESAME SEAFOOD KEBABS

SERVES 6

These bright, colourful kebabs are a perfect treat for children and adults alike.

170g/6oz Young's Seafood Sticks, defrosted and cut into chunks
200g/7oz Young's Extra Large Prawns, defrosted
2 small courgettes
6 cherry tomatoes
1 yellow pepper, seeded and cut into chunks
Watercress to garnish

Marinade
15ml/1 tbsp dry sherry
15ml/1 tbsp soy sauce
15ml/1 tbsp sesame oil
Finely grated rind and juice of 1 lemon
15ml/1 tbsp sesame seeds

---

1. Mix together all the marinade ingredients and toss the seafood sticks and prawns in the mixture to coat evenly. Cover and chill for 2 hours.

STEP 1

2. Cut thin strips from the courgette skin then cut them into thick slices. Thread into twelve skewers with the seafood sticks, prawns, tomatoes and pepper chunks.

STEP 2

3. Cook the kebabs on a moderately hot barbecue for about 6 minutes, basting with the marinade and turning occasionally.

STEP 3

Cook's Notes

⌚ TIME: Preparation takes about 10 minutes, plus 2 hours for marinating and approximately 6 minutes for cooking.

? VARIATION: Can also be cooked under a medium grill for 10 minutes.

CONTINENTAL CRAB SALAD
SERVES 6

This exotic salad is the perfect starter for dinner parties.

170g Young's Dressed Crab, defrosted
50g/2oz frisée, torn into pieces
50g/2oz escarole, torn into pieces
50g/2oz radicchio, torn into pieces
25g/1oz Feuille de chêne, torn into pieces
1 avocado
30ml/2 tbsps lemon juice
15ml/1 tbsp white wine vinegar
75ml/5 tbsps sunflower oil

2. Peel, stone and thinly slice the avocado, toss it in 1 tbsp lemon juice to prevent it turning brown and add to the salad mixture.

STEP 2

1. Tear the frisée, escarole, radicchio and Feuille de chêne into pieces, place in a bowl and toss lightly to mix.

3. Mix vinegar, oil, white and brown crab meat and remaining lemon juice together and spoon onto the salad. Toss lightly before serving.

STEP 1

STEP 3

Cook's Notes

⏱ TIME: Preparation takes about 15-20 minutes.

◯ SERVING IDEA: Ideal as a first course or main meal accompaniment.

SPECKLED SALMON SALAD
SERVES 6

Light and tasty, this is the perfect summer salad.

2 × 85g/3oz Young's Scottish Smoked Salmon
  slices, defrosted
1 cucumber
3 spring onions
2 tbsps chopped, fresh tarragon
5ml/1 tsp tarragon vinegar
15ml/1 tbsp lime juice
60ml/4 tbsps natural yogurt
Salt and freshly ground pepper
Sprigs of tarragon and slices of lime to garnish

1. Cut the smoked salmon, cucumber and spring onions into thin julienne strips and place in a mixing bowl with the chopped tarragon.

2. Mix the vinegar, lime juice, yogurt and seasoning together and pour over the salad. Stir gently to mix and place in a serving bowl.

STEP 2

STEP 1

STEP 2

Cook's Notes

TIME: Preparation takes about 20 minutes.

SERVING IDEAS: Ideal as a starter. Garnish with sprigs of tarragon and lime slices. Serve with brown bread or crusty French bread.

SCOTTISH SALMON BAKE

SERVES 4

Fresh herbs and almonds complement the salmon perfectly in this impressive dish.

10ml/2 tsps sunflower oil
2 x 227g/8oz Young's Scottish salmon steaks, defrosted
60ml/2fl oz dry white wine
2 tbsps freshly chopped dill or 2 tsps dried dill
Salt and freshly ground black pepper
50g/2oz Cheddar cheese, grated
15g/½oz flaked almonds, lightly roasted
Fresh dill to garnish

1. Heat the oven to 190°C/375°F/Gas Mark 5. Brush an ovenproof dish with oil and arrange the salmon steaks in the dish. Pour over the wine and sprinkle with dill. Season with salt and pepper.

2. Mix the cheese and almonds together and divide among the steaks. Cover loosely with foil and bake for 20 minutes.

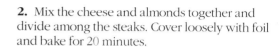

STEP 2

STEP 1

STEP 2

Cook's Notes

⏱ TIME: Preparation takes about 10 minutes, plus 20 minutes for baking.

◯ SERVING IDEAS: Garnish with sprigs of fresh dill and serve with new potatoes and green vegetables.

POACHED SALMON STEAKS WITH TARRAGON MAYONNAISE

SERVES 2

This elegant dish is certain to be a success whenever it is served.

600ml/1 pint water
300ml/½ pint dry white wine
30ml/2 tbsps white wine vinegar
Pinch of salt
6 black peppercorns
1 small onion, sliced
1 small carrot, sliced
2 x 227g/8oz Young's Scottish salmon steaks, defrosted
4 sprigs fresh tarragon or 4 tsps dried tarragon

Sauce
75ml/5 tbsps mayonnaise
125g/4oz low-fat soft cheese
10ml/2 tsps lemon juice
1 tbsp freshly chopped tarragon or 1 tsp dried tarragon
Fresh tarragon to garnish

1. Put the water, wine, vinegar, salt and peppercorns into a large shallow pan with the onion and carrot, simmer for 15 minutes. Place the steaks in the pan with a sprig of tarragon or 1 tsp of dried tarragon on each.

2. Gently poach for 5 minutes. Leave in the liquid until completely cold, then transfer to a serving plate and garnish with fresh tarragon.

STEP 2

3. Mix the sauce ingredients together, adding a little of the poaching liquid if it is too thick, season with salt and pepper. Serve with the salmon.

STEP 1

STEP 3

Cook's Notes

TIME: Preparation takes 10 minutes, plus 20 minutes for cooking.

SERVING IDEAS: Garnish with fresh tarragon.

GRILLED CITRUS TROUT

SERVES 4

An exciting dish that will liven up any meal.

1 grapefruit
Juice of 1 orange
1 small onion, finely chopped
30ml/2 tbsps white wine vinegar
4 sprigs fresh thyme or 1 tsp dried thyme
4 sprigs fresh parsley
Salt
2.5g/½ tsp black peppercorns, roughly crushed
4 Young's Rainbow Trout, defrosted
A little oil for brushing
15g/1 tsp cornflour
Fresh sprigs of thyme and orange zest strips to
  garnish

1. Finely grate the grapefruit rind into a shallow dish and mix with the orange juice, onion, vinegar herbs and seasonings.

2. Put the fish into the dish and coat with the marinade, spooning it into the cavity of each trout. Set aside for 30 minutes.

STEP 2

3. Meanwhile, segment the grapefruit, catching the juices in a dish. Remove the trout from the marinade and make two criss cross cuts in the skin on both sides. Place on a grill pan lined with foil and brush with oil. Cook under a moderate heat for about 7 minutes on each side.

STEP 3

4. Strain the marinade into a saucepan, blend in the cornflour and add the reserved gapefruit juice. Heat, stirring all the time, until thickened.

STEP 4

5. Add any cooking juices from the fish and serve with the trout, garnished with the grapefruit segments, sprigs of fresh thyme and strips of orange zest.

Cook's Notes

⏱ TIME: Preparation takes about 15 minutes, plus 30 minutes for marinating, 15 minutes for grilling.

◯ SERVING IDEA: Serve with new potatoes.

❓ VARIATION: Pink grapefruit may be used if preferred.

MINTED TROUT WITH CUCUMBER SAUCE

SERVES 4

This stylish dish is simply delicious.

Half a cucumber
Salt and freshly ground black pepper
4 Young's Rainbow Trout, defrosted
8 sprigs fresh mint
1 lemon, sliced
25g/1oz butter
225g/8oz Greek yogurt
Extra fresh mint to garnish

1. Halve the cucumber lengthwise, scoop out the seeds, then grate onto a double thickness of kitchen paper. Sprinkle with ½ teaspoon of salt and set aside.

STEP 1

2. Heat the oven to 190°C/375°F/Gas Mark 5.

3. Season the inside of the trout with salt and pepper and place two sprigs of mint in each cavity. Using a sharp knife, make 3 deep diagonal slits into one side of each trout.

4. Cut the lemon slices in half and insert into slits.

STEP 4

5. Place the trout in an ovenproof dish, dot with butter, then cover with foil and bake for 20 minutes.

6. Put the yogurt into a pan, stir in the cucumber and heat gently. Remove the mint from the trout, place on a warm serving dish and serve garnished with fresh mint. Serve the sauce separately.

STEP 6

Cook's Notes

🕐 TIME: Preparation takes about 10 minutes and baking takes about 20 minutes.

◎ SERVING IDEA: Serve with new potatoes and seasonal vegetables.

SOUFFLE OMELETTE WITH PRAWN STIR-FRY

SERVES 2

Makes a really quick lunch or supper dish.

6 eggs (size 3), separated
45ml/3 tbsps water
Salt and freshly ground black pepper
A little cooking oil

Filling
15ml/1 tbsp cooking oil
¼ green pepper, seeded and very finely sliced
½ small onion, very finely sliced
50g/2oz Chinese beansprouts
100g/4oz Young's peeled prawns, defrosted
5ml/1 tsp soy sauce

1. Beat the egg yolks with water and seasoning. Whisk whites until stiff, stir a tbsp into yolks and fold in the rest.

STEP 1

2. Lightly oil a 25cm/10-inch frying pan and heat over a medium hob. Pour in egg mixture and cook for 10 minutes until omelette is just set and the base lightly browned. Finish off under a hot grill.

STEP 2

3. Heat the oil for the filling in a fry pan and stir-fry the pepper and onions for 2 minutes. Add the beansprouts, prawns and soy sauce. Toss well together and use to fill the omelette. Fold the omelette over and serve at once.

STEP 3

Cook's Notes

TIME: Preparation takes about 10 minutes, with 25 minutes for cooking.

PRAWN AND PEPPER CASSEROLE

SERVES 8

This adaptable dish is suitable for almost any occasion.

1 large onion, sliced
15g/½oz butter
15ml/1 tbsp cooking oil
2 green peppers, 2 red peppers and 1 yellow
    pepper all seeded and cut into small squares
150ml/¼ pint fish stock or water
Pinch mixed dried herbs
Salt and freshly ground black pepper
680g/1½lbs Young's cooking prawns, defrosted
Parsley sprigs to garnish

1. Gently fry onion in the butter and oil for 2-3 minutes. Add the peppers. Fry gently for a further 2-3 minutes.

STEP 1

2. Add remaining ingredients, except prawns. Bring to the boil, cover and simmer for 30 minutes. Add the prawns and cook for a further 2-3 minutes and serve immediately.

STEP 1

STEP 2

Cook's Notes

TIME: Preparation takes 10 minutes, plus 40-45 minutes for cooking.

SERVING IDEA: Serve hot with rice or noodles.

PRAWN LASAGNE

SERVES 6-8

A new twist to a classic dish.

225g/8oz lasagne verdi
1 stick celery
1 carrot
1 small onion
1 clove garlic
15ml/1 tbsp corn oil
700ml/1¼ pints passato (Italian sieved tomatoes)
45ml/3 tbsps chopped fresh oregano
Salt and pepper to taste
454g/1lb Young's Peeled Prawns, defrosted
400g/14oz can artichoke hearts, chopped
225g/8oz mozzarella cheese
Extra oregano sprigs to garnish

1. Cook the lasagne in plenty of boiling water for 8-10 minutes, until just soft. Remove from pan and drain singly to prevent sticking.

2. Very finely chop the celery, carrot and onion. Crush the garlic and fry these gently in the oil until soft, but not brown. Turn off the heat and add the passato, oregano and seasoning.

3. Place a little of the tomato mixture in the base of large lasagne dish. Place one third of the lasagne of top, then add half the prawns and chopped artichokes. Cover with tomato sauce. Repeat with more lasagne, seafood, and sauce, finishing with a few tablespoons of sauce.

STEP 3

4. Slice the cheese very thinly. Arrange in a layer on top of the dish. Place in the centre of a preheated oven at 200°C/400°F/Gas Mark 6, for 40-50 minutes.

STEP 2

STEP 4

Cook's Notes

TIME: Preparation takes about 20 minutes, plus 40-60 minutes for cooking.

SERVING IDEAS: Serve with salad and garlic bread.

GINGERED CRAB SALAD
SERVES 4

Surprise your guests with this unusual starter.

2 × 170g/6oz Young's Dressed Crab, defrosted and
   drained
15ml/1 tbsp cider vinegar
15ml/1 tbsp soy sauce
1 tbsp freshly grated root ginger
Salt and freshly ground black pepper
15ml/1 tbsp vegetable oil
2 sticks celery, sliced
50g/2oz button mushrooms, wiped and sliced
4 spring onions, topped, tailed and sliced
¼ cucumber
Parsley sprigs to garnish

1. In a large bowl combine the dressed crab,
vinegar, soy sauce, ginger and seasoning.

2. Heat the oil in a frying pan, add the celery,
mushrooms and spring onions and stir-fry for 2
minutes. Add the vegetables to the crab mixture
and mix well.

STEP 2

3. Cut the cucumber in half lengthways, scoop out
the seeds with teaspoon and slice the cucumber to
form half moon shapes. Add cucumber to the
mixture. Garnish with parsley sprigs before
serving.

STEP 1

STEP 3

Cook's Notes

⏱ TIME: Preparation 15 minutes, plus 6-8
minutes for cooking.

◻ SERVING IDEA: Spoon into cleaned crab
shells or crisp lettuce leaves.

PRAWN-STUFFED TROUT

SERVES 4

A sophisticated dish which can be prepared in practically no time.

Stuffing
15ml/1 tbsp vegetable oil
50g/2oz mushrooms, wiped and sliced
50g/2oz fresh white breadcrumbs
200g/7oz Young's Extra Large Prawns, defrosted
½ tsp freshly chopped thyme
Salt and freshly ground black pepper
½ (size 3) egg, beaten

4 Young's Rainbow Trout, defrosted

Sauce
Knob of butter
15g/1 tbsp plain flour
125ml/¼ pint milk
30ml/2 tbsps single cream
Salt and freshly ground black pepper
1 tbsp freshly chopped mixed herbs
Whole prawns and fresh dill to garnish

1. Heat the oil in a frying pan and fry the mushrooms for 2 minutes until golden. Remove from pan and place in a mixing bowl.

2. Add the breadcrumbs, prawns, thyme, seasoning and egg and mix thoroughly. Divide the mixture between the trout and stuff each trout well.

3. Place the trout in a large frying pan and pour in enough water to just cover the trout. Bring to the boil and leave to simmer for 6-8 minutes.

4. Remove from pan and carefully remove the skin, leaving the head and tail in tact. Place the trout on serving plates and keep warm.

STEP 4

5. Melt the butter in a saucepan, stir in the flour and cook for 1 minute. Gradually add the milk until all is absorbed. Bring to the boil and stir until thickened.

6. Stir in the cream, seasoning and herbs. Pour the sauce over the trout and serve immediately, garnished with whole prawns and dill.

STEP 2

Cook's Notes

TIME: Preparation takes about 20 minutes, plus 30 minutes for cooking.

SERVING IDEA: Serve with seasonal vegetables.

SARDINE AND TOMATO SALAD

SERVES 4

A tasty dish which is quick and easy to make.

30ml/2 tbsps vegetable oil
1 tsp finely chopped fresh marjoram
Salt and freshly ground black pepper
454g/1lb Young's Sardines, defrosted
2 little gem lettuces, washed and separated
2 beef tomatoes, sliced
1 red onion, peeled and sliced
¼ cucumber, sliced

Dressing
60ml/4 tbsps vegetable oil
60ml/4 tbsps white wine vinegar
10ml/2 tsps Dijon mustard
Salt and freshly ground black pepper
2 tbsps freshly chopped marjoram
Sprigs of fresh marjoram to garnish

1. Mix together the oil, marjoram and seasoning in a small bowl and brush liberally over the sardines. Place under a preheated moderate grill for 10 minutes turning and basting occasionally.

STEP 1

2. Arrange the lettuce, tomato, onion and cucumber on serving plates.

STEP 2

3. Combine the oil, wine vinegar, mustard, seasoning and marjoram in a screw top jar, shake well to mix then pour over the salad. Garnish with marjoram before serving.

STEP 3

Cook's Notes

TIME: Preparation takes 15 minutes, plus 10 minutes for cooking.

LEMON SOLE GOUJONS WITH CRAB DIP

SERVES 2

Goujons are always popular and are the perfect addition to a buffet table.

200g/7oz Young's Lemon Sole Goujons
170g/6oz Young's Dressed Crab, defrosted
30ml/2 tbsps double cream
10ml/2 tsps lemon juice
Salt and freshly ground black pepper
2 tbsps freshly chopped dill
Fresh green peppercorns, to garnish

2. In a bowl mix together the dressed crab, cream, lemon juice, seasoning and dill.

STEP 2

1. Cook the sole goujons as directed on the packet.

STEP 1

3. Arrange the sole goujons on a serving plate and serve with the crab dip garnished with green peppercorns.

STEP 3

Cook's Notes

TIME: Preparation takes about 10 minutes, plus 8-10 minutes for cooking.

MUSTARD POACHED SALMON STEAKS

SERVES 4

In this recipe salmon is enlivened with the tangy taste of mustard.

2 × 227g/8oz Young's Scottish Salmon Steaks, defrosted
225ml/8fl oz white wine vinegar
Juice of 1 lemon
1 small onion, peeled and finely chopped
5g/1 tsp caster sugar
60g/4 tbsps wholegrain mustard
Salt and freshly ground black pepper

STEP 2

1. Place the salmon steaks in a large frying pan. Cover with the wine vinegar, lemon juice, chopped onion, sugar, mustard and seasoning.

flakes. Remove salmon from the pan, carefully skin and keep warm. Boil remaining liquid fiercely until slightly reduced.

STEP 1

STEP 2

2. Bring to the boil then simmer, basting occasionally, for 5-8 minutes until the salmon

3. Place salmon steaks on warmed serving plates and pour over cooking liquor. Serve immediately.

Cook's Notes

TIME: Preparation takes 10 minutes, plus 8-10 minutes for cooking.

SERVING IDEA: Serve with potatoes and crisp green salad.

SPICY SEAFOOD SELECTION

SERVES 4

The perfect party dip or appetiser.

175g/7oz Young's Lemon Sole Goujons
227g/8oz Young's Golden King Prawns
15ml/1 tbsp vegetable oil
1 large onion, peeled and finely chopped
225g/8oz tomatoes, peeled, seeded and chopped
90ml/6 tbsps mayonnaise
30ml/2 tbsps Worcestershire sauce
15ml/1 tsp Tabasco Sauce
2 tbsps chopped herbs
Salt and freshly ground black pepper
Tomato and coriander sprigs to garnish

STEP 2

1. Cook the goujons and prawns as directed on the packet.

3. In a bowl mix together the mayonnaise, Worcestershire sauce, Tabasco sauce, herbs and seasoning to taste. Stir in the tomato and onion mixture.

STEP 1

2. Heat the oil in a frying pan, add the onion and fry for 2 minutes. Add the prepared tomatoes and cook for a further 5 minutes until soft. Blend the mixture in a liquidiser or food processor until smooth.

STEP 3

4. Serve the goujons and prawns with the spicy dip garnished with tomato and coriander sprigs.

Cook's Notes

⌐ TIME: Preparation takes 15 minutes, plus 8 minutes to cook seafood and about 8 minutes to make dip.

GRILLED PRAWNS WITH SPICY PESTO MARINADE

SERVES 4

These spicy prawns are the perfect addition to a buffet table or barbecue.

200g/7oz Young's Extra Large Prawns, defrosted
Wooden cocktail sticks
60ml/4 tbsps sesame oil
30ml/2 tbsps sherry
2 tsps freshly grated root ginger
2 cloves garlic, peeled and crushed
Salt and freshly ground black pepper
1 green chilli, seeded and finely chopped
2 tbsps basil, shredded
Lemon pieces and fresh basil sprigs to garnish

1. Thread the prawns alternately onto wooden cocktail sticks. In a jug combine the oil, sherry, ginger, garlic, seasoning, chilli and basil.

STEP 1

STEP 2

3. Remove prawns from marinade and place under a low preheated grill. Grill for 5 minutes, turning occasionally and basting with remaining marinade.

STEP 3

2. Place the prawns on sticks in a large shallow dish and pour over the sauce. Leave to marinate for 30 minutes.

4. Serve immediately.

Cook's Notes

🕐 TIME: Preparation takes about 15 minutes, plus 30 minutes for marinating and a further 5 minutes for grilling.

❓ VARIATION: Can also be barbecued.

PRAWN AND FRENCH BEAN SALAD

SERVES 4

An unusual salad, perfect for unexpected guests.

450g/1lb tomatoes, skinned, seeded and diced
200g/7oz Young's Extra Large Prawns, defrosted
100g/4oz French beans, topped and tailed and cut
    into 2.5cm/1-inch length
50g/2oz fennel tops, sliced
1 tbsp chives, snipped
1 tbsp basil, shredded
1 clove garlic, peeled and crushed
30ml/2 tbsps sherry vinegar or white wine vinegar
1 tbsp wholegrain mustard
Salt and freshly ground black pepper

Cutting beans

1. Combine the tomatoes, prawns, beans, fennel, chives, basil, garlic, vinegar and mustard in a large bowl.

2. Season to taste and toss until well mixed. Serve immediately.

Preparing tomatoes

STEP 2

Cook's Notes

TIME: Preparation takes about 15 minutes, plus 5 minutes for mixing.

SERVING IDEA: Serve with artichoke leaves or crisp lettuce leaves.

CHINESE-STYLE SOUP

SERVES 4-6

Serve up a taste of China with this delicious soup.

1.16 litres/2 pints chicken stock
175g/6oz sweetcorn kernels
1 tsp freshly grated root ginger
4 spring onions, topped, tailed and sliced
170g/6oz Young's Seafood Sticks, defrosted and
   shredded
50g/6oz Young's Peeled Prawns, defrosted
60ml/4 tbsps dry sherry
Salt and freshly ground black pepper
30ml/2 tbsps cornflour
Carrot flowers for garnish

1. Place the chicken stock in a saucepan and bring to the boil. Add the sweetcorn, root ginger, spring onions, seafood sticks and prawns.

2. Add the sherry and seasoning to taste. Blend the cornflour in a small bowl with enough cold water to form a smooth paste.

STEP 2

3. Stir the cornflour paste into the soup and simmer gently for 5 minutes, stirring until slightly thickened.

STEP 1

STEP 3

Cook's Notes

TIME: Preparation about 10 minutes, plus a further 10 minutes for cooking.

SERVING IDEA: Serve as a first course or a main meal garnished with carrot flowers.

THAI PRAWN SALAD

SERVES 4

This easy-to-prepare salad is ideal as a starter or served as part of a buffet meal.

1 green apple, cored and finely grated
45ml/3 tbsps lemon juice
45ml/3 tbsps lime juice
1 shallot, peeled and sliced
1 tbsp freshly chopped coriander
1 tbsp freshly chopped mint
10ml/2 tsps soy sauce
1 garlic clove, peeled and crushed
1 tsp fresh red chillies, seeded and chopped
400g/14oz Young's Peeled Prawns, defrosted
4 spring onions, topped, tailed and sliced
Salt and freshly ground black pepper
Spring onion curls to garnish

1. In a large mixing bowl mix together the apple, lemon and lime juice, shallot, coriander, mint, soy sauce, garlic, chilli, prawns, spring onions and seasoning.

STEP 1

2. Chill in a refrigerator until required then serve in crisp lettuce leaf shells.

Grating apple

STEP 2

Cook's Notes

TIME: Preparation takes 10-15 minutes.

SALMON STEAKS WITH TOMATO AND BASIL SAUCE

SERVES 4

Salmon steaks are always a welcome treat and here they are even more inviting with a tangy sauce.

---

2 × 227g/8oz Young's Scottish Salmon Steaks, defrosted
300ml/½ pint white wine
Salt and freshly ground black pepper
30ml/2 tbsps vegetable oil
1 small onion, peeled and finely chopped
1 clove garlic, peeled and crushed
450g/1lb tomatoes, skinned, seeded and chopped
1 stick celery, sliced
Pinch sugar
2 tbsps freshly shredded basil leaves
Basil leaves to garnish

---

1. Place salmon steaks in a frying pan, pour over wine and season to taste. Bring to the boil, reduce the heat and leave to simmer for 8-10 minutes until the salmon flakes.

STEP 1

2. Remove the salmon from the pan and keep warm. Boil the remaining wine fiercely until reduced to 150ml/¼ pint. Pour into a jug.

3. Heat the oil in the frying pan and add the onion and garlic. Fry for 2 minutes then add the tomatoes and celery. Cook for a further 5 minutes until tomato and celery are soft.

STEP 3

4. Add the sugar, seasoning and wine and simmer for a few minutes. Remove from heat and liquidise until smooth. Stir in the shredded basil and serve with the salmon steaks on warmed serving plates.

STEP 4

Cook's Notes

TIME: Preparation takes about 30 minutes plus 10-15 minutes for cooking.

SERVING IDEA: Serve with new potatoes and seasonal green vegetables.

WALDORF CRAB

SERVES 4-6

The ideal summer salad.

60ml/4 tbsps mayonnaise
30ml/2 tbsps natural yogurt
1 Granny Smith's apple
2 celery stalks
25g/1oz walnuts, roughly chopped
10 Young's Seafood Sticks, defrosted
5-6 lettuce leaves

1. Mix together mayonnaise and yogurt.

STEP 1

2. Core and chop the apple, chop the celery and add to the dressing with the walnuts.

STEP 2

3. Cut each seafood stick into 3, then stir into the other ingredients. Arrange lettuce leaves around the edge of a serving dish. Spoon the salad into the centre and refrigerate for 1 hour before serving.

STEP 3

Cook's Notes

TIME: Preparation time takes about 10 minutes.

SERVING IDEA: Serve as a starter.

INDEX

Photography by Peter Barry
Recipes Prepared and Styled by Helen Burdett
Designed by Judith Chant
Edited by Jillian Stewart